Clean Eating:

Lose Weight for Life—7 Days to a Perfect Body Following the Clean Eating Diet (2nd Edition)

By Danyale Lebon

Disclaimer

© Copyright 2014 by Danyale Lebon - All rights reserved.

This document is geared towards providing exact and reliable information in regards to the topic and issue covered. The publication is sold with the idea that the publisher is not required to render accounting, officially permitted, or otherwise, qualified services. If advice is necessary, legal or professional, a practiced individual in the profession should be ordered.

- From a Declaration of Principles which was accepted and approved equally by a Committee of the American Bar Association and a Committee of Publishers and Associations.

In no way is it legal to reproduce, duplicate, or transmit any part of this document in either electronic means or in printed format. Recording of this publication is strictly prohibited and any storage of this document is not allowed unless with written permission from the publisher. All rights reserved.

The information provided herein is stated to be truthful and consistent, in that any liability, in terms of inattention or otherwise, by any usage or abuse of any policies, processes, or directions contained within is the solitary and utter responsibility of the recipient reader. Under no circumstances will any legal responsibility or blame be held against the publisher for any reparation, damages, or monetary loss due to the information herein, either directly or indirectly.

Respective authors own all copyrights not held by the publisher.

The information herein is offered for informational purposes solely, and is universal as so. The presentation of the information is without contract or any type of guarantee assurance.

The trademarks that are used are without any consent, and the publication of the trademark is without permission or backing by the trademark owner. All trademarks and brands within this book are for clarifying purposes only and are the owned by the owners themselves, not affiliated with this document.

Table of Contents

DISCLAIMER 2

INTRODUCTION 7

PART 1 9

CHAPTER 1: WHAT IS CLEAN EATING? 10
    THE GUIDING PRINCIPLES BEHIND CLEAN EATING 11
    THE DIFFERENT WAYS OF DOING CLEAN EATING 14
        Method 1: Four Times a Day Meal Plan 14
        Method 2: Going Organic/3x a Day Meal Plan 15
        Method 3: 6 Small Meals Daily 15

CHAPTER 2: HELPING YOU GET INTO CLEAN EATING FOR LOSING WEIGHT 17
    TIPS ON DOING YOUR GROCERY SHOPPING 17
        Tip #1: Perimeter Shopping 17
        Tip #2: Use Minimal Ingredients 18
        Tip #3: How to Read Food Labels 18
    TIPS FOR GETTING STARTED ON CLEAN EATING 19

PART 2 22

CHAPTER 3: CLEAN EATING DAY 0 23

    Cleaning the Ref and Freezer 24
    Clean the Pantry 25
    7-Day Meal Plan 26
    Grocery List 28
    Meal Preparation 30

CHAPTER 4: CLEAN EATING DAY 1 32
    Breakfast: Sunflower Seeds and Arugula Garden Salad 33
    Lunch: Sweet Potatoes Oven Fried 34
    Dinner: Slow Cooked Pot Roast 35

CHAPTER 5: CLEAN EATING DAY 2 38
    Breakfast: Warm Salad with Brussels Sprouts and Nuts 38
    Lunch: Easy Stir Fried Chicken 40
    Dinner: Lemony and Garlicky Shrimp 41

CHAPTER 6: CLEAN EATING DAY 3 43
    Breakfast: Chicken Breasts with Stuffing 43
    Lunch: Slow Cooked Salsa Chicken 45
    Dinner: Pesto and Lemon Halibut 46

CHAPTER 7: CLEAN EATING DAY 4 48
    Breakfast: Fruity and Cheesy Quesadilla 48
    Lunch: Pesto Pasta and Shrimps 49
    Dinner: Blue Cheese, Fig and Arugula Salad 50

CHAPTER 8: CLEAN EATING DAY 5 52
    Breakfast: Pan Fried Tuna with Herbs and Nut 52

LUNCH: BUTTERED SCALLOPS IN WINE 54
DINNER: SLOW COOKED CREAMY CHICKEN SOUP 55

CHAPTER 9: CLEAN EATING DAY 6 57
CHILI BUTTERED SHRIMP 57
LUNCH: CUCUMBER AND TOMATO SALAD 59
DINNER: TENDERLOIN STEAKS WITH CARAMELIZED ONIONS 60

CHAPTER 10: CLEAN EATING DAY 7 62
BREAKFAST: CURRY SALMON WITH MUSTARD 62
LUNCH: CUCUMBER, CHICKEN AND MANGO WRAP 64
DINNER: CREAMY CARROT CHOWDER 65

CHAPTER 11: CLEAN EATING EXTRA RECIPES 68
GARDEN SALAD WITH CRAISINS AND BALSAMIC VINEGAR 68
CHEESE QUESADILLA 69
FRUITY ASPARAGUS-QUINOA SALAD 70
POTATO CHOWDER 72
BREAD DIP AND TOPPING GALORE 73
MACARONI SOUP 74

PREVIEW OF "FRUIT FUSION: FRUIT INFUSED SMOOTHIES FOR ULTIMATE WEIGHT LOSS AND DETOX (FRUIT INFUSED WATER COMPLIMENTARY EDITION)" 77
SAMPLE RECIPE: DETOXIFYING SUPER GREEN SMOOTHIE 79

CHECK OUT MY OTHER BOOKS 81

Introduction

First off, I would like to thank you for buying this eBook titled: "Clean Eating: Lose Weight for Life: 7 Days to a Perfect Body Following the Clean Eating Diet." Next, I would like to congratulate you for taking that first step to living a healthy lifestyle.

If you have bought this book, out of curiosity—then you will not be disappointed because you will learn a lot about clean eating here. You will be introduced to the concept of clean eating—although I am sure that you may already have an idea about it; whether you already know it or not. Clean eating is not a "NEW" concept, in fact it has been touted everywhere but the difference lies on the many ways that you can achieve a healthy lifestyle. Clean eating in a way has consolidated all the possible ways that you could introduce a healthy eating way into your lifestyle.

This eBook is segregated into two parts. The first part is where you will learn the basics, such as what clean eating is all about and how to go about clean eating plus some tips and tricks. After learning what clean eating is all about, you are ready to proceed with Part 2. In part two, you will not only have a 1-week meal plan, where you are provided with a 7-day meal plan complete with recipes to help you kick start a healthy lifestyle and lose unwanted weight fast; you will have a full week of clean eating plan too! This means that instead of preparing, haranguing and getting stressed for a BIG makeover—I have made it easy for you by laying out the groundwork and all you have to do is follow.

Enjoy!

PART 1

Learn the ropes fast on clean eating. Understand the rules and driving concepts behind clean eating to fast track your knowledge of this healthy lifestyle. Once you finish reading this part, you are guaranteed to have an in-depth knowledge of clean eating.

Chapter 1: What is Clean Eating?

You may or may not have heard of clean eating but this is the current buzz word in the world of health-conscious consumers. Clean eating is basically an idea that puts focus on unprocessed, whole and healthy foods. The name may be catchy and somewhat new to a lot of us, but the guiding principles behind this lifestyle choice have been around for decades. Also clean eating is not just about losing weight but it is also about eating healthy in order to have more energy, glowing skin, disease free and a whole lot of other benefits. As many other writers have written, if you eat junk food—your body will show the results of these unhealthy junk foods like obesity, long-term illnesses, unhealthy skin and many more undesirable health effects. Therefore, clean eating tells us that food is "THE" ticket to good health.

At the simple level, clean eating is more centered on the process in between your plate and the origin of your food, like how it was grown. Clean eating is not about restricting your food caloric intake or restricting some types of food. As we have mentioned above, clean eating is simply about whole and unprocessed foods.

The Guiding Principles behind Clean Eating

There are so many guiding principles about clean eating that you will find online, however most of them can easily be categorized under the following groups:

- **Get Moving** – You need to do some exercise each day not only because you want to lose weight but also because for your health. Daily exercise not only helps jumpstart the weight loss process but it also helps you build muscles which make it possible for you to burn more energy even at rest. Further, exercise helps keep your bones, lungs and heart strong and healthy.

- **Don't drink your calories** – high calorie drinks like coffee rich in cream and milk, sodas and juices. Coffee per se is not high in calories but if you are fond of buying that Starbucks Caramel Macchiato, chances are the caramel, whipped cream and milk added into it can rack up to 400 calories without fully satisfying your appetite. The same is true for juices and sodas. These drinks are very high in meaningless calories without providing you any nutritional benefit—just hordes of sweetness and a handful few vitamins.

- **Space out Your Meals** – when we say meals, even snacks is counted as meals. So whatever type of clean eating method you are in, it is always best to have at least 4 different meals in a day, that's breakfast, lunch, snack and dinner. This will inhibit you from getting hungry easily and avoid overeating. Spacing out your meals equally also ensures that your blood sugar levels stay steady all throughout the day.

- **Minimize or totally eliminate processed foods in your diet** – when we say processed foods these are foods that are packaged, canned, bagged or in a box. If you can create your own pasta from scratch, then that would be great—but if you can't then try to choose those that are made organically. This is the reason why we placed "minimize" on the heading because some newbie dieters easily get demotivated when they find that changing their diet is difficult, so why not do it little by little, right? Further, processed foods are those that have high sugar, salt and preservative content that is a known cause for diabetes, high blood pressure and cancer, respectively.

- **Watch out for sugar, salt and fat in your meals** – you might think that this is hard but once you eliminate or minimize your processed food from your diet, this part becomes easier. All you have to do is check your cooking or meals for too much use of sugar or other sweeteners, too much use of salt, soy sauce and other condiments and fat. Try to choose lean cuts of meats and minimize the use of oils when cooking.

- **Have some fat, carbohydrate and protein in a meal** – with the many health diets that we have heard of or read about we are always cautioned about eating protein and fats. But, in fact for a healthy and balanced diet you still need protein and fat because these have important roles in our body for it to perform certain functions optimally. Protein helps build muscles and it also helps keep you feeling full. While fats on the other hand provide flavor to food and helps in absorption of oil soluble vitamins. Just make sure that you space out your protein and fat consumption while keeping it to a minimum.

- **Opt for unrefined foods rather than refined foods** – examples of these choices are: rather than going for refined table sugar, go for dehydrated sugar cane juice, maple syrup or honey. Instead of going for refined grains go for quinoa, amaranth, millet, or brown rice. Do not forget your vegetables/legumes and beans as these are also good sources of important vitamins and nutrients.

- **Lower your Alcohol Intake** – if you are going into clean eating, then you would also have to clean what you are drinking. Meaning if you can't let go of your alcohol vice, and then make sure that you stay within the recommended limits and that's 5-oz of wine for women a day and twice the size for men. Other recommended limits are: 12-oz of beer and 1.5-oz of liquor. Stay away from mixed drinks as these are sure to be high in sugar.

- **Increase your organic fruit and veggie intake** – not just any fruit or veggie will do, when I say fruits and vegetables that only means one thing: ORGANIC. As I have said earlier and repeating again, clean eating is also about the process of how food reaches your plate. If it is not organic, then it underwent gazillions of insecticide sprays making it "unclean." Further, when talking about vegetables, it doesn't only mean green and leafy ones. You can easily add veggies to your cooking by making use of onions, garlic, ginger, tomatoes and many more to any dish. And not to mention, bumping up your fruit and veggie intake provides you with lots of vitamins and minerals.

The Different Ways of Doing Clean Eating

There are actually three different methods of eating clean, and we will tackle each of them below in detail.

Method 1: Four Times a Day Meal Plan

In this clean eating method, you have breakfast, lunch and dinner meals plus one snack. The idea is to space out the meals into four hour intervals, instead of the frequent feeding meals of two to three hours. This idea was presented by Jillian Michaels who reported that with a frequent meal at two to three hour intervals (which is around 6 meals a day) your blood sugar levels are always on the rise which makes you more at risk for getting diabetes.

Method 2: Going Organic/3x a Day Meal Plan

Another clean eating approach is going organic, this means that people opt for food with no harmful chemicals, genetically modified ingredients (GMO's) or other unnatural elements. So, basically this approach is on general and overall health and wellbeing; and not on losing weight, but it can be incorporated to your clean eating weight loss regime too. Remember, natural foods do not leave the higher volumes of waste in the body like their processed counterparts do and as a result, a diet containing highly processed foods can cause more difficulty in losing weight for good. Furthermore, in this method of avoiding processed foods dieters only eat 3 meals a day or only when the need to eat arises.

Method 3: 6 Small Meals Daily

This is the common clean eating method used by a lot of dieters. People who are on a clean eating diet under this method basically eat dishes with fewer ingredients which ensure that they know all the ingredients that they eat are unprocessed and unrefined. In this method, they eat six small meals in a day—breakfast, lunch, two snacks and they divide their dinner into two in order to have 6 small meals in a day. They enjoy eating lots of vegetables and fruits. They also enjoy unprocessed and unrefined grains plus meat. They are also careful to read the labels on the food that they buy.

Chapter 2: Helping You Get Into Clean Eating For Losing Weight

So how do you get started into clean eating? Easy! I have set out a few steps for you to follow and you will be on your way to clean eating in no time. First things first, when you go on a clean eating regimen, you need to change your habits and one of them is your grocery habits.

Tips on Doing Your Grocery Shopping

If you believe that adding changes to your grocery shopping just by reading the labels, then you are in for a whole day of buying. Reading all the food labels is impractical and simply means that you have not fully embrace letting go of processed foods. As I have mentioned over and over again, in clean eating processed foods simply have no room in your pantry.

Tip #1: Perimeter Shopping

I urge you to avoid the aisles when doing your grocery shopping because all the fresh foods are found on the perimeter. I suggest that you buy fresh fruits, fresh vegetables and fresh meat and seafood. Don't worry;

whipping up a delicious dish in your kitchen does not require you to be Einstein's daughter, I have solved your problem with some simple recipes in the next chapter.

Tip #2: Use Minimal Ingredients

If you are a newbie cook or a newbie clean eater, I suggest that you begin creating dishes that contain few ingredients so that you can easily trace the roots of your food. And if you need to buy a lot of different ingredients in one grocery shopping trip or multiple stores you might get fed up with what to choose and simply leave the store frustrated and never touch any clean eating guide ever again. I urge you to start small because you can easily fit clean eating grocery shopping in your time with fewer ingredients—this is your getting to know the ingredients phase. From there, you can start adding to your list and sooner or later you will be a guru on which food abides by clean eating and which does not. Eventually with practice, grocery shopping will be a breeze for you!

Tip #3: How to Read Food Labels

The next tip I am going to share with you is how to read food labels. Okay, not all of us have the time and effort to pursue a full-time career in cooking so you can have a chosen few processed foods to splurge on. Let's take for example a jar of spaghetti sauce. So, how do you know if it's okay for clean eating? First, you would want to look on the list of "Ingredients" and check it one by one. For example, if the ingredients list of the jar of spaghetti sauce says: garlic, olive oil, tomatoes and cheese. Do you use garlic in your kitchen? Yes. What about olive oil? Yes. Tomatoes? Yes. Cheese? Yes. Then, it definitely falls under clean eating.

But, what about if the ingredients list says: garlic, olive oil, tomatoes, cheese and maltodextrin? Do you use maltodextrin in your home cooking? Or do you even go, buy and look for maltodextrin in the grocery? NO and NO. So, this jar of spaghetti sauce does not fall under the clean eating category, so scrap it out.

Tips for Getting Started on Clean Eating

Now, ready yourself to embrace the clean eating lifestyle with these strategies:

- **Give yourself time to adjust** – do not expect yourself to perfect clean eating right away. Don't let mistakes put you off the right path. I tell you that you will soon encounter problems with buying foods that are not clean; you can easily return it to the store or just chalk it up to experience and learn from it. You may find it hard to cook, but just be patient everything begins with a learning curve and it all tapers down one way or another.

- **Get a small cooler** – if you are on the move all the time because of work, having a cooler with you ensures that you have clean foods with you all the time. You can easily prepare your meals the night before and in the morning, just pop them into the cooler with some ice bags and you're good to go anywhere without getting anxious on what or where to eat next.

- **Make a grocery list** – having a grocery list ensures that you are within your budget and you only need to buy what is written in your list. But, maybe you can add a few more stuff if it still fits the budget.

- **Shopping day is preparation day too** – to make it easy for the whole week, after doing the grocery, I start segregating the food into containers so that I know that what I bought will last me the whole week. Especially for the meat, I cut them up; sometimes I start marinating them, put them in containers and freeze them. So that when the time to cook them comes along, all I have to do is defrost and start cooking. This is also true with cut up meat, just defrost and start cooking.

- **Preparing food ahead of time** – what I do to buffer on those occasions when I simply have no energy to make meals is to prepare foods that freeze well like casseroles. I make them after doing my grocery shopping. If the need arises, I just pop the casserole in the oven and leave it there for an hour to defrost and reheat while I do my thing. If I am really in a hurry, I pop it in the microwave defrost for ten minutes, heat on high for 5 minutes intervals and I have some really delicious main meal in a jiffy!

- **Dividing Your Meal** – it seems too onerous to prepare 6 different meals in a day, so what I do is prepare 3 meals (that you normally eat) and divide the serving in two. So that you can eat your meal every two to three hours. And if that's not enough, you can throw in a serving of your favorite fruit.

PART 2

To help you get started in your journey to a big change, I have decided to do all the hard work and provide you a step by step plan that's good for 1-week to get you into the clean eating band wagon. Inside part 2, aside from providing you with meal plans for the day, I am also adding tips, tricks and details on how to go about the clean eating process to make the transition easier for you.

Chapter 3: Clean Eating Day 0

Before you can start changing your eating habits and overall lifestyle in order to fully accommodate the clean eating lifestyle, you have to set "DAY 0."

During this day, you have to prime up your mind that it's going to be a bit of work and heartache. You need to clean out your refrigerator, throw away items that are not suited to your lifestyle and likewise with your pantry too. Don't worry; I'll give you specific tips later on as we begin. I promise to stick with you through thick and thin of Day 0.

So to summarize, during Day 0 you will need to clean out your ref and pantry for food items that do not belong to clean eating. Next, check out the meal plan I have laid out for you for the incoming 7 days. And don't worry because the recipes are already included plus the grocery list too! All you have to do is print out the list, drive to the grocery and shop. And your last task before Day 0 ends is to prepare meals. There are meal recipes that I have included which you can prepare and freeze ahead of time so that you can just reheat it—I am not giving you any reason to stop and procrastinate because you don't have time or you have so many things to do and cooking takes the backseat. But, with reheating food? I don't think that would work.

Knowing what you have to do on Day 0, this means you really have to psyche and prepare yourself about this day. Pick a day where you don't have work to do and let your family know what you want to do for that day. You can even enlist them for help.

Cleaning the Ref and Freezer

Why do you need to clean the ref? It's because all those years of undesirable eating habits are reflected in your ref. I am sure you have loads of foods in there that are high in sugar, high in fat, contain preservatives and maybe moldy foods? You have to clean them up and throw them away. This way, you are sending out a message to yourself and your family that you mean business. By throwing away these nasty foods, you won't be tempted by them each time you open your ref—the same goes for your pantry.

So, here are some quick rules to follow:

- Read the labels of the food inside the ref – if it contains ingredients that you do not normally use, and then throw it away. Remember my tip to you on how to read food labels? Put that concept into play here. If that salad dressing says it contains phosphoric acid, potassium sorbate, calcium disodium EDTA, potato maltodextrin and any other tongue twisting ingredient—I'm sorry but you have

to throw it out. Even if only one of these ingredients is included, you have to scrap it out.
- Keep only the food that's duly approved by clean eating – this means that keep only the frozen meat, fresh fruits, fresh vegetables, fresh milk and other fresh and organic foods inside your ref.
- Frozen meat – if you no longer remember when you have bought that piece of frozen meat, I suggest throwing it away rather than risk getting sick from it.
- Make a list of what you have – list all the foods that's inside your ref, you would need this before you go on your grocery shopping.
- Do clean your ref properly – since you are changing to clean eating and most foods in this lifestyle is fresh and organic, this means it gets spoiled easily. And if your ref is not clean, your foods are MORE prone to spoilage. You can place coffee beans in a cup and leave it inside your ref to keep it smelling good. You can also make use of an opened small box of baking soda left in the ref to absorb odors.

Clean the Pantry

When it comes to cleaning the pantry, you need to remember that most foods here are processed foods. Therefore, time and effort must be put into reading the food labels. If money and budget is a problem for you and letting go of all these canned foods is not economical, you can save some. And when saving some, do try to retain canned foods that only have 2 or 3 preservatives or added chemicals. The rest you would have to let go of them.

In order not to waste these foods, you can donate them to shelters—at least something good comes out of it. Further, do not try to consume the retained canned foods in a week's time. Try to use it just once or twice a week until such time that it's all used up.

Also take note of the expiration dates of the foods in your pantry, throw away those that have already expired.

Lastly, list down the food items left in the pantry, alongside your list of foods in the ref.

7-Day Meal Plan

So, before you go on your grocery trip, do check out the clean eating meal plan that I have setup just for you. Familiarize yourself with the food that you will be eating for the next week so that when you do your grocery shopping, you would have an idea of what to look for and not just blindly follow a list of items.

	Monday	**Tuesday**	**Wednesday**	**Thursday**
Breakfast	Sunflower Seeds and Arugula	Warm Salad with	Chicken Breasts with	Fruity and Cheesy Quesadilla

		Garden Salad	Brussels Sprouts and Nuts	Stuffing	
Lunch	*Sweet Potatoes Oven Fried	*Easy Stir Fried Chicken	**Slow Cooked Salsa Chicken	Pesto Pasta and Shrimps
Dinner	**Slow Cooked Pot Roast	Lemony and Garlicky Shrimp	Pesto and Lemon Halibut	Blue Cheese, Fig and Arugula Salad

*can be prepared ahead of time
**Can be made on the day early in the morning

	Friday	**Saturday**	**Sunday**
Breakfast	Pan Fried Tuna with Herbs and Nut	Chili Buttered Shrimp	Curry Salmon with Mustard
Lunch	Buttered Scallops in Wine	Cucumber and Tomato Salad	Cucumber, Chicken and Mango Wrap
Dinner	* & **Slow Cooked Creamy Chicken Soup	Tenderloin Steaks with Caramelized Onions	Creamy Carrot Chowder

*can be prepared ahead of time
**Can be made on the day early in the morning

Grocery List

Before you go on your grocery shopping trip, print out the list below and crush out the items that you already have in your pantry and ref or maybe just add or subtract from how much you need to buy.

Items	How Many	Items	How Many
Fresh Produce		**Baking**	
basil	1 bunch	whole wheat flour	1 pound bag
baby arugula	3 big bags		
bell pepper, red	1 large piece	**Bakery**	
bell pepper, orange	1 large piece	bread crumbs	1 small bag
Brussels sprouts	¾ lbs		
carrots	1 or 2 lb bag	**Spices**	
cilantro	1 bunch	black pepper	1 small bag (4 oz)
cucumber	2 medium pieces	chili powder	1 small bag (4 oz)
figs	1 pint	sunflower seeds	1 small bag (4 oz)
garlic	2 bulbs	mustard grain	1 small bag (4 oz)
ginger	5-inch piece	thyme, dried	1 small bag (4 oz)
grape	0.5 lb	turmeric	1 small bag

tomatoes			(4 oz)
green onions	4 bunches	walnuts	1 small bag (4 oz)
lemon	4 pcs		
lettuce	1 head	**Deli**	
mango	2 pcs	blue cheese, crumbled	4-oz
mint	1 bunch	feta cheese	4-oz
mushrooms	1 pack	Asiago cheese	4-oz
orange	1 big piece	Jack cheese	4-oz
onion, red	4 medium pieces	Parmesan cheese	6-oz
parsley	1 bunch		
pasta, whole wheat, angel hair	4-oz	**Condiments**	
salt	1 small bottle	salad dressing, Italian style	1 small bottle
salsa	1 medium bottle	salad dressing, ranch	1 small bottle
spinach	2 big bags	soy sauce	1 small bottle
sweet potatoes	4 medium pieces		
tangerine	2 pieces	**Grocery**	
tarragon	1 bunch	Balsamic Vinegar	1 small bottle
tomatoes	3 big tomatoes	butter	1 bar
		chicken	good for 7

		broth	cups
Meat/Seafood/Poultry		coconut oil	1 small bottle
beef, chuck roast boneless	2.5 lbs	gravy, beef	good for 1 cup
beef, tenderloin steaks	4 pcs (around 24-oz total)	honey	1 small bottle
chicken breast	16 large pieces	Mustard, Dijon	1 small bottle
halibut	4 pieces (6-oz each)	olive oil	1-liter bottle
salmon	4 pieces around 24-oz total	olives	1 small jar
sea scallops	1.5 lbs	soy sauce	
shrimps, peeled and deveined	5 lbs	tortilla whole grain	9-inch round
tuna	24 oz or 2 fillets	yogurt, 2% Greek style	1 big tub, good for 2 cups
		white wine	1 bottle

Meal Preparation

Now that you are done with grocery shopping, it's time to segregate and prepare ahead of time the meals that you will be preparing for the next 7 days. Put away all grocery items into the pantry, the fresh produce into its designated places inside the ref and leave behind the meat products. Why? Because, you need to re-pack the meat, especially the chicken into 1 zip lock bag per recipe. This way, you do not have to bring out all the chicken and defrost and return the unused chicken back into the freezer, doing it this way will cause your meat, poultry and fish to spoil faster.

Some quick tips:

- You can place the following inside the freezer right away—meaning no need to re-bag them as they are good for one recipe: boneless chuck roast, halibut filets, sea scallops, tenderloin steaks, tuna filets, and salmon filets.

- What you need to re-bag are the chicken and the shrimps into the following:
    1. Chicken: 1 bag with 1 piece chicken breast; 2 bags with 2 pieces of chicken breast each; 1 bag of 3 pieces chicken breast; and 1 bag of 8 pieces chicken breast.
    2. Shrimps: 2 bags of 1.5 lbs of shrimp each and 1 bag of 2 lbs of shrimps.

- Recipes that you need or can prepare today, after your grocery trip:
    1. Sweet Potatoes Oven Fried
    2. Easy Stir Fried Chicken
    3. Slow Cooked Creamy Chicken Soup

Chapter 4: Clean Eating Day 1

As part of this clean eating program for weight loss, do not forget to insert daily 30 minute exercises into your clean eating regimen. If you do not have a full 30 minutes to give to an exercise routine, you can break it up into ten minute short exercises throughout the day.

Here's one tip to insert exercise for day one: instead of getting that coffee break, skip it and instead go for a short ten minute exercise called wall sits. Just find an empty room to do this quick exercise. To start the position, lean on your back flat against a wall with your hands completely relaxed on your side and your feet firmly planted on the floor at least a foot away from the wall. Slowly, slide down until your thighs are parallel to the floor. It's like sitting on the air, with your back up against the wall. Hold the position for as long as you can. Do not forget to breathe as you hold this position. You can hold the position loner if you breathe faster as it gets tougher.

Wall sits makes use of half of your body's muscle tissues that are found on your back, abdominals, gluteus and leg muscles.

Breakfast: Sunflower Seeds and Arugula Garden Salad

Coconut oil is rich in medium chain triglycerides (MCT) which helps improve energy expenditure as much as 5% within a 24-hour timeframe—which means more weight loss! These MCTs can also affect body weight positively by reducing appetite.

Servings per Recipe: 6
Calories per Serving: 81
Fat: 3.1 g
Protein: 1.6 g
Carbohydrates: 13.1 g

Ingredients:
¼ tsp black pepper
¼ tsp salt
1 tsp fresh thyme, chopped
2 tbsps sunflower seeds, toasted
2 cups red grapes, halved
7 cups baby arugula, loosely packed
1 tbsp coconut oil
2 tsps honey
3 tbsps red wine vinegar
½ tsp stone-ground mustard

Directions:

1) In a small bowl, whisk together mustard, honey and vinegar. Slowly pour oil as you whisk.
2) In a large salad bowl, mix thyme, seeds, grapes and arugula.
3) Drizzle with dressing and serve.

Lunch: Sweet Potatoes Oven Fried

*can be prepared ahead of time

Sweet potatoes are rich in fiber. It also has a low glycemic index rating and low-glycemic foods stay longer in your stomach thereby helping you control your hunger.

Servings per Recipe: 7
Calories per Serving: 176
Fat: 2.5 g
Protein: 2.5 g
Carbohydrates: 36.6 g

Ingredients:
1 small garlic clove, minced
1 tsp grated orange rind
1 tbsp fresh parsley, chopped finely
¼ tsp pepper
¼ tsp salt
1 tbsp olive oil

4 medium sweet potatoes, peeled and sliced to ¼-inch thickness

Directions:

1) In a large bowl mix well pepper, salt, olive oil and sweet potatoes.
2) In a greased baking sheet, in a single layer arrange sweet potatoes.
3) Pop in a preheated 400ºF oven and bake for 15 minutes, turnover potato slices and return to oven. Bake for another 15 minutes or until tender.
4) Meanwhile, mix well in a small bowl garlic, orange rind and parsley, sprinkle over cooked potato slices and serve.
5) You can store baked sweet potatoes in a lidded container and just microwave whenever you want to eat it. Do consume within 3 days.

*To prepare ahead of time, follow direction number 1. Then place sweet potatoes and marinade inside a zip lock bag and freeze. To cook, just remove from the freezer, defrost for around 4 minutes as you wait for your oven to heat. Then follow instructions starting on directions #2.

Dinner: Slow Cooked Pot Roast

**Can be made on the day early in the morning

Chuck roast is considered as a lean meat and in order to digest protein, our body needs calories. And out of all the food groups, meat needs more energy or calories to be expended just to digest it—thus chuck roast is considered as a calorie burning food.

Servings per Recipe: 6
Calories per Serving: 385
Fat: 22 g
Protein: 23.9 g
Carbohydrates: 20.8 g

Ingredients:
5 whole carrots, peeled
2 cups water
3 tbsps Italian style salad dressing
3 tbsps ranch dressing
1 cup beef gravy
Pepper and salt to taste
2.5 lbs boneless chuck roast
¼ cup whole wheat flour
1 onion, sliced thinly
3 tbsps soy sauce
2 tbsps honey

Directions:

1) Grease slow cooker with cooking spray and arrange onion slices on bottom.

2) Season chucks roast with pepper and salt to taste. Cover with flour and put on top of onions.
3) In a medium bowl, mix water Italian dressing, ranch dressing, gravy, and soy sauce. Pour into slow cooker.
4) Add carrots. Cook for 8 hours or until beef is tender on low setting.
5) Evenly divide into 6 portions and store in 6 different lidded containers for a quick and easy meal.

**This recipe can be made early in the morning before you go to work or run errands out of the house.

Chapter 5: Clean Eating Day 2

Aside from sticking to the meal plan I have created for you, remember that you also have to insert at least 30 minutes of vigorous activity—and don't ever forget this.
If you don't have time, you can actually cut up the 30 minutes into ten minute exercise segments. My exercise tip for the second day is to have a 'move more' mindset. This means that try to incorporate exercise movements as you do mundane chores. For example, as you talk to someone on the phone, a client or friend perhaps, you can walk around the office or house to burn off energy or even do some squats. Another idea would be to take the stairs instead of using the elevator or escalator. You can also insert some exercises as you watch the TV. The key is to stay active and on the move as much as you can rather than sitting as much as you can.

Breakfast: Warm Salad with Brussels Sprouts and Nuts

Brussels sprouts are a great food for losing weight because it is a filling food without packing too much calories. One great news too is that it is rich in protein, vitamins and minerals to help your body work optimally.

Servings per Recipe: 6
Calories per Serving: 71
Fat: 3.1 g
Protein: 3.5 g
Carbohydrates: 8.9 g

Ingredients:
½ oz. Asiago cheese, shaved
1 ½ tbsps toasted walnuts, finely chopped
1/8 tsp black pepper
¼ tsp salt
¾ lb Brussels sprouts
1/3 cup fresh bread crumbs
1 garlic clove, minced
1 ½ tsps olive oil, divided

Directions:

1) Slice Brussels sprouts in half then separate the leaves from the cores. Cut the cores in quarters and set aside.
2) On medium fire, place a large nonstick saucepan and heat 1 tsp oil. Sauté garlic for a minute.
3) Add breadcrumbs and sauté for another minute or until lightly browned. Transfer to a bowl.
4) In same pan, add remaining oil and cook Brussels sprouts until crisp tender around 8 minutes.

5) Transfer to serving bowl, pour in breadcrumb mixture and toss to mix.
6) Garnish with cheese and nuts before serving.

Lunch: Easy Stir Fried Chicken

*can be prepared ahead of time

When trying to shed pounds, eating lean chicken breast is a great way to do so because even when on a weight loss diet your body still needs protein and chicken is a good source of protein without extra calories.

Servings per Recipe: 3
Calories per Serving: 252
Fat: 10 g
Protein: 32 g
Carbohydrates: 7 g

Ingredients:
1 tbsp soy sauce
1 tbsp virgin coconut oil
¼ medium onion, sliced thinly
¼ lb brown mushrooms
1 large orange bell pepper
2 7-oz skinless and boneless chicken breast

Directions:

1) On medium high fire, place a nonstick saucepan and heat coconut oil.
2) Add soy sauce, onion powder, mushrooms, bell pepper and chicken.
3) Stir fry for 8 to 10 minutes. Remove from pan and serve.
4) You can store in 3 separate lidded containers for 3 quick meals in the week.

Dinner: Lemony and Garlicky Shrimp

Shrimps are a good source of protein with fewer calories than its counterparts. Four large shrimps contain minimal fat, 6 grams of protein at only 30 calories.

Servings per Recipe: 4
Calories per Serving: 257
Fat: 4 g
Protein: 46 g
Carbohydrates: 7 g

Ingredients:
Chopped cilantro for garnish
¼ tsp chili powder – optional
Juice of 3 lemons
10 cloves garlic, finely chopped

2 lbs jumbo shrimp

1 tbsp olive oil

Directions:

1) On medium fire, place a nonstick large fry pan and heat oil.
2) Add garlic and stir fry until lightly browned, around 5 minutes.
3) Add shrimps; stir fry for two minute on high fire and lower fire to medium.
4) Cook shrimp uncovered for another 5 minutes, to allow water to evaporate.
5) If there's still water in pan, continue cooking and stirring until water evaporates.
6) Turn off fire and add pepper and juice of lime. Stir to mix well.
7) Transfer to a serving platter and garnish with cilantro.
8) Serve and enjoy.

Chapter 6: Clean Eating Day 3

Here are more quickie exercise routines that you can use during the day:

- While cooking dinner and waiting for that pot to boil, why not do some quick standing pushups. This is easily done by standing at an arm's length from the kitchen counter, then place both palms of hands against the edge of the counter, lean your body forward and let your arms support you as you push yourself up.
- As you go out to pick your paper or get the mail, why not make a quick brisk walk around the block.
- Do some 5 or 10 minute jumping jack. Did you know that 10 minutes of jumping jacks can help you burn as much as 90 calories?

Breakfast: Chicken Breasts with Stuffing

*can be prepared ahead of time

Based on studies, olives have shown to breakdown fats inside our body's fat cells—this means that eating olives help you get rid of belly fat. Plus, it helps reduce your sensitivity to hunger.

Servings per Recipe: 8
Calories per Serving: 210
Fat: 5.9 g
Protein: 35.2 g
Carbohydrates: 1.8 g

Ingredients:
8 pcs of 6-oz boneless and skinless chicken breasts
1 tbsp minced fresh basil
2 tbsps finely chopped, pitted Kalamata olives
¼ cup crumbled feta cheese
1 large bell pepper, halved and seeded

Directions:

1) In a greased baking sheet place bell pepper with skin facing up and pop into a preheated broiler on high. Broil until blackened around 15 minutes. Remove from broiler and place right away into a re-sealable bag, seal and leave for 15 minutes.
2) After, peel bell pepper and mince. Preheat grill to medium high fire.
3) In a medium bowl, mix well basil, olives, cheese and bell pepper.
4) Form a pocket on each chicken breast by creating a slit through the thickest portion; add 2 tbsps bell pepper mixture and seal with a wooden pick. (At

this point, you can stop and freeze chicken and just thaw when needed for grilling)
5) Season chicken breasts with pepper and salt.
6) Grill for six minutes per side, remove from grill and cover loosely with foil and let stand for 10 minutes before serving.

Lunch: Slow Cooked Salsa Chicken

**Can be made on the day, early in the morning.

Salsa is a very low calorie food that instantly perks up a simple dish. It can easily substitute high calorie and high fat dressings or condiments for potatoes, burgers and sandwiches.

Servings per Recipe: 6
Calories per Serving: 138
Fat: 2.5 g
Protein: 22.1 g
Carbohydrates: 4.6 g

Ingredients:
2 cups salsa
3 large boneless, skinless chicken breasts

Directions:

1) Place chicken into slow cooker and cover completely with salsa. Cook for 4.5 hours on low setting.
2) Strain chicken and begin shredding chicken with fork.
3) Mix shredded chicken with salsa and enjoy.
4) You can freeze the dish in 6 separate containers for 6 quick meals during the week.

Dinner: Pesto and Lemon Halibut

Halibut is an oily fish that's rich in omega-3 fatty acids. This fatty acid helps in reducing triglyceride levels and slows arterial plaque growth. Halibut is rich in protein with less calories compared to other protein rich foods.

Servings per Recipe: 4
Calories per Serving: 283
Fat: 13 g
Protein: 38.7 g
Carbohydrates: 1.4 g

Ingredients:
1 tbsp fresh lemon juice
1 tbsp lemon rind, grated
2 garlic cloves, peeled
2 tbsps olive oil
¼ cup Parmesan Cheese, freshly grated

2/3 cups firmly packed basil leaves
1/8 tsp freshly ground black pepper
¼ tsp salt, divided
4 pcs 6-oz halibut fillets

Directions:

1) Preheat grill to medium fire and grease grate with cooking spray.
2) Season fillets with pepper and 1/8 tsp salt. Place on grill and cook until halibut is flaky around 4 minutes per side.
3) Meanwhile, make your lemon pesto by combining lemon juice, lemon rind, garlic, olive oil, Parmesan cheese, basil leaves and remaining salt in a blender. Pulse mixture until finely minced but not pureed.
4) Once fish is done cooking, transfer to a serving platter, pour over the lemon pesto sauce, serve and enjoy.

Chapter 7: Clean Eating Day 4

If you are always tied to a desk in your office—no worries, I still have a lot of exercising tips that you can do.

You can do some quick 5 or 10 minute Upward pushups. So, here's how to do this exercise: place your palms against your desk, at least shoulder breadth apart. Then push yourself up with your hands supporting your weight. Repeat as many times as you can. You can also do this exercise against a wall.

With this exercise, you are stabilizing your shoulder blades and strengthen your back muscles and the large latissimus dorsi muscle.

Breakfast: Fruity and Cheesy Quesadilla

Mango is a fibrous fruit that boosts digestion thereby burning additional calories. It also rich in nutrients and vitamins which also aids in making the body feel fuller.

Servings per Recipe: 1
Calories per Serving: 165
Fat: 9 g

Protein: 7 g
Carbohydrates: 15 g

Ingredients:
¼ cup hand grated jack cheese
1 tbsp chopped fresh cilantro
½ cup finely chopped fresh mango
1 large whole-grain tortilla

Directions:

1) In a medium bowl, mix cilantro and mango.
2) Place mango mixture inside tortilla and top with cheese.
3) Pop in a preheated 350ºF oven and bake until cheese is melted completely around 10 to 15 minutes.

Lunch: Pesto Pasta and Shrimps

Grape tomatoes tastes sweet yet is a low calorie food. It is also rich in fiber, lycopene, vitamins and minerals which are helpful in losing weight.

Servings per Recipe: 4
Calories per Serving: 320
Fat: 11 g
Protein: 31.4 g

Carbohydrates: 23.6 g

Ingredients:
¼ cup shaved Parmesan Cheese
1 cup halved grape tomatoes
¼ cup pesto, divided
1 ¼ lbs large shrimp, peeled and deveined
4-oz angel hair pasta, cooked, rinsed and drained

Directions:

1) On medium high fire, place a nonstick large fry pan and grease with cooking spray.
2) Add tomatoes, pesto and shrimp. Cook for 15 minutes or until shrimps are opaque, while covered.
3) Stir in cooked pasta and cook until heated through.
4) Transfer to a serving plate and garnish with Parmesan cheese.

Dinner: Blue Cheese, Fig and Arugula Salad

Figs add sweetness to this dish but not the added calories. It is also rich in fiber which promotes fullness thereby helping you reach your weight loss goals.

Servings per Recipe: 4
Calories per Serving: 219

Fat: 10 g
Protein: 2.5 g
Carbohydrates: 25.5 g

Ingredients:
Pepper and salt to taste
3 tbsps olive oil
1 tsp Dijon mustard
3 tbsps Balsamic Vinegar
¼ cup crumbled blue cheese
2 bags arugula
1 pint fresh figs, quartered

Directions:

1) Whisk thoroughly together pepper, salt, olive oil, Dijon mustard, and balsamic vinegar to make the dressing. Set aside in the ref for at least 30 minutes to marinate and allow the spices to combine.
2) On four serving plates, evenly arrange arugula and top with blue cheese and figs.
3) Drizzle each plate of salad with 1 ½ tbsps of prepared dressing.
4) Serve and enjoy.

Chapter 8: Clean Eating Day 5

Here is another exercise tip while ensconced in your office. This exercise helps relieve lower backache, neck pain and sciatica. This exercise is wonderful for toning your waist and oblique abdominals. It is also a good stretching exercise for your hips, shoulders and spine. To do the seated chair twist, start by inhaling deeply, position your left hand on the outside of your right knee and place your right hand on the armrest and twist your torso to the left and hold for five breaths. Repeat at least three times and do the same on the other side and you can repeat alternately.

Breakfast: Pan Fried Tuna with Herbs and Nut

Tuna is a great food to include in your weight loss plan because it packs a lot of protein, vitamins and minerals that your body needs without packing too much calories. Thus, you do not need to eat a lot of caloric rich food just to provide your body with the nutrients it needs.

Servings per Recipe: 4

Calories per Serving: 277
Fat: 9.7 g
Protein: 42 g
Carbohydrates: 4.2 g

Ingredients:
4 pieces of 6-oz Tuna steak cut in half
½ tsp ground pepper, divided
½ tsp sea salt, divided
½ tsp fennel seeds, chopped finely
1 tbsp olive oil
2 tbsps fresh mint, chopped finely
2 tbsps red onion, chopped finely
¼ cup fresh tangerine juice
¼ cup almonds, chopped finely

Directions:

1) Mix fennel seeds, olive oil, mint, onion, tangerine juice and almonds in small bowl. Season with ¼ each of pepper and salt.
2) Season fish with the remaining pepper and salt.
3) On medium high fire, place a large nonstick fry pan and grease with cooking spray.
4) Pan fry tuna until desired doneness is reached or for one minute per side.
5) Transfer cooked tuna in serving plate, drizzle with dressing and serve.

Lunch: Buttered Scallops in Wine

Scallops are rich in tryptophan which is an essential amino acid that helps in regulating appetite. This means that scallops is high in satiety factor.

Servings per Recipe: 4
Calories per Serving: 225
Fat: 8 g
Protein: 28.6 g
Carbohydrates: 4.7 g

Ingredients:
Black pepper – optional
1 tbsp butter
¼ tsp salt
1 ½ tsps chopped fresh tarragon
½ cup dry white wine
1 tbsp olive oil
1 ½ lbs large sea scallops

Directions:

1) On medium high fire, place a large nonstick fry pan and heat oil.
2) Add scallops and fry for 3 minutes per side or until edges are lightly browned. Transfer to a serving plate.

3) On same pan, add salt, tarragon and wine while scraping pan to loose browned bits.
4) Turn off fire, add butter and stir until melted.
5) Pour sauce over scallops and serve.

Dinner: Slow Cooked Creamy Chicken Soup

*Can be made ahead of time
**Can be made on the day early in the morning

According to a clinical study led by Dr. Michael Zemel, eating yogurt helps you achieve flat abs better because its calcium content helps in signaling your fat cells to pump out less cholesterol helping you shed off weight.

Servings per Recipe: 7
Calories per Serving: 130
Fat: 4 g
Protein: 18 g
Carbohydrates: 6 g

Ingredients:
1 lb skinless and boneless chicken breasts
2 cups unsweetened almond milk
1 tsp balsamic vinegar
4 tbsps whole wheat flour
4 cups chicken broth
Chopped fresh parsley
Pepper and salt to taste

¼ of medium onions, sliced thinly
1 clove garlic, minced
¾ cup plain Greek yogurt

Directions:

1) In a slow cooker, add chicken broth.
2) Whisk in almond milk and vinegar.
3) Add chicken, garlic and onions. Cook for 4 to 6 hours on low setting or until chicken is tender.
4) Once cooked, remove chicken breast and shred.
5) Whisk in pepper, salt, and Greek yogurt into soup inside the slow cooker until well combined.
6) Return chicken to slow cooker and mix well.
7) Serve equally into seven bowls and garnish with parsley.
8) Serve and enjoy.

*This recipe can be stored in the freezer for up to a month. In the ref for up to 3 days.

Chapter 9: Clean Eating Day 6

Often times we feel that our day or time is wasted with waiting for our doctor during an appointment, waiting for our children to finish some lesson related practice and the list goes on. Make use of this time with the following exercises:

- If you are waiting for your kid during a soccer game, why not do some exercise yourself? Do a brisk walk around the park.
- While waiting for a doctor's appointment, ask the secretary how much time you've got and use it to do some brisk walking around the building or up and down some flight of stairs.
- And best of all, why not bring your kid to the park? Throw some ball together and do make a run for that fly ball. This way, you are killing two birds with one stone—spending quality time with the family while getting fit in an enjoyable manner.

Chili Buttered Shrimp

As recommended by Dr. Oz, chili helps you lose weight by boosting your metabolism!

Servings per Recipe: 4
Calories per Serving: 186
Fat: 7 g
Protein: 27.5 g
Carbohydrates: 2 g

Ingredients:
½ tsp salt
2 tbsps butter
2 tbsps fresh lime juice
1 tsp chili powder
1 ½ lbs large shrimp, peeled and deveined
¾ cup chopped green onions, divided

Directions:

1) On medium high fire, place a large nonstick fry pan and grease with cooking spray.
2) Sauté ½ cup onions until soft and translucent around 4 to 5 minutes.
3) Add chili powder and shrimp, sauté until cooked around 4 minutes.
4) Turn off fire and add salt, butter and lime juice. Stir until butter is melted.
5) Serve and enjoy.

Lunch: Cucumber and Tomato Salad

Eat as much as you can with this salad recipe, aside from its yummy goodness but also because of its thylakoids content which help you curb your craving for unhealthy foods—also known as hedonic hunger.

Servings per Recipe: 4
Calories per Serving: 34
Fat: 0.3 g
Protein: 1.3 g
Carbohydrates: 7.1 g

Ingredients:
Ground pepper to taste
Salt to taste
1 tbsp fresh lemon juice
1 onion, chopped
1 cucumber, peeled and diced
2 tomatoes, chopped
4 cups spinach

Directions:

1) In a salad bowl, mix onions, cucumbers and tomatoes.
2) Season with pepper and salt to taste.
3) Add lemon juice and mix well.
4) Add spinach, toss to coat, serve and enjoy.

Dinner: Tenderloin Steaks with Caramelized Onions

Tenderloin is another lean beef cut. It helps increase the body's thermogenesis thereby increasing metabolism.

Servings per Recipe: 4
Calories per Serving: 289
Fat: 11.4 g
Protein: 32.5 g
Carbohydrates: 12.6 g

Ingredients:
4 pcs of 4-oz beef tenderloin steaks, trimmed
¼ tsp ground black pepper
1 tsp dried thyme
½ tsp salt, divided
2 tbsps honey
2 tbsps red wine vinegar
1 large red onion, sliced into rings and separated

Directions:

1) On medium high fire, place a large nonstick fry pan and grease with cooking spray.
2) Add onion, cover and cook for three minutes.
3) Add ¼ tsp salt, honey and vinegar. Stir to mix and reduce fire to medium low.

4) Simmer until sauce has thickened around 8 minutes. Stir constantly. Turn off fire.
5) In an oven safe pan, grease with cooking spray add beef. Season with pepper, thyme and remaining salt.
6) Pop into a preheated broiler on high and broil for 4 minutes. Remove from oven and turnover tenderloin pieces. Return to oven and broil for another 4 minutes or until desired doneness is achieved.
7) Transfer to a serving plate and pour onion sauce over.
8) Serve and enjoy.

Chapter 10: Clean Eating Day 7

We are already at the end of our clean eating plan and how fast tie flies. This time, I will be teaching you sneaky exercises while watching TV or just relaxing around and spending time with the family.

- While watching your favorite TV show, why not lift some small weights?
- Do you hate those time consuming TV ads? Why not jog in place while these ads drone on and on. Just 5-minutes of jogging can help you burn as much as 45 calories.
- If you haven't tried it yet, do play some dancing games on Wii with the family. Not only does it help you lose weight, it's a great way for you bond with your family.

Breakfast: Curry Salmon with Mustard

Salmon is a lean protein that provides you with a handful of amino acids at lesser calories compared to other protein packed food. Thereby helping you prevent eating more.

Servings per Recipe: 4
Calories per Serving: 324
Fat: 18.9 g
Protein: 34 g
Carbohydrates: 2.9 g

Ingredients:
4 pcs 6-oz salmon fillets
¼ tsp salt
1/8 tsp garlic powder or 1 clove garlic minced
¼ tsp ground red pepper or chili powder
¼ tsp ground turmeric
1 tsp honey
2 tsps whole grain mustard

Directions:

1) In a small bowl mix well salt, garlic powder, red pepper, turmeric, honey and mustard.
2) Preheat oven to broil and grease a baking dish with cooking spray.
3) Place salmon on baking dish with skin side down and spread evenly mustard mixture on top of salmon.
4) Pop in the oven and broil until flaky around 8 minutes.

Lunch: Cucumber, Chicken and Mango Wrap

This recipe is a great way to lose weight because you have all the right types of food in the right amounts at a low calorie count to boot.

Servings per Recipe: 1
Calories per Serving: 350 calories
Fat: 10 g
Protein: 21 g
Carbohydrates: 65 g

Ingredients:
1 whole wheat tortilla wrap
1-inch thick slice of chicken breast around 6-inch in length
½ of ripe mango
2 to 4 lettuce leaves
½ of a medium cucumber cut lengthwise
1 tbsp salad dressing of choice
2 tbsps whole wheat flour
Salt and pepper to taste
2 tbsps oil for frying

Directions:

1) Slice a chicken breast into 1-inch strips and just cook a total of 6-inch strips. That would be like two strips of chicken. Store remaining chicken for future use.

2) Season chicken with pepper and salt. Dredge in whole wheat flour.
3) On medium fire, place a small and nonstick fry pan and heat oil. Once oil is hot, add chicken strips and fry until golden brown around 5 minutes per side.
4) While chicken is cooking, place tortilla wrap in oven and cook for 3 to 5 minutes. Then remove from oven and place on a plate.
5) Slice cucumber lengthwise, use only ½ of it and store remaining cucumber. Peel cucumber, cut into quarter and remove pith. Place the two slices of cucumber on the tortilla wrap, 1-inch away from the edge.
6) Slice mango and store the other half with seed. Peel the mango without seed, slice into strips and place on top of the cucumber on the tortilla wrap.
7) Once chicken is cooked, place chicken beside the cucumber in a line.
8) Add cucumber leaf, drizzle with salad dressing of choice.
9) Roll the tortilla wrap, serve and enjoy.

Dinner: Creamy Carrot Chowder

Carrots are nutrient and vitamin rich food. Plus, it contains a good amount of fiber to help you feel full at less the amount of calories compared to other foods.

Servings per Recipe: 8
Calories per Serving: 47
Fat: 1.6 g
Protein: 2.2 g
Carbohydrates: 6.5 g

Ingredients:

8 fresh mint sprigs
½ cup 2% Greek Style Plain yogurt
1 tsp fresh ginger, peeled and grated
2 cups chicken broth
1 lb baby carrots, peeled and cut into 2-inch lengths
1/3 cup sliced green onions
2 tsps olive oil

Directions:

1) On medium fire, place a medium heavy bottom pot and heat oil.
2) Sauté shallots until tender around 2 minutes.
3) Add carrots and sauté for another 4 minutes.
4) Pour broth, cover and bring to a boil. Once soup is boiling, slow fire to a simmer and cook carrots until tender around 22 minutes.
5) Add ginger and continue cooking while covered for another eight minutes.
6) Turn off fire and let it cool for 10 minutes.
7) Pour mixture into blender and puree. If needed, puree carrots in batches then return to pot.

8) Heat pureed carrots until heated through around 2 minutes.
9) Turn off fire and evenly pour into 8 serving bowls.
10) Serve and enjoy. Or you can store in the freezer in 8 different lidded containers for a quick soup in the middle of the week.

Chapter 11: Clean Eating Extra Recipes

I have added extra recipes here that will help you clean out your ref and pantry. Most of the dishes here make use of the extra food items from the grocery list that I have provided you. Plus, not only will these clean eating recipes help you clean out your ref and pantry, it's delicious and low calorie to boot. Just perfect for your clean eating weight loss plans.

Garden Salad with Craisins and Balsamic Vinegar

Servings per Recipe: 1
Calories per Serving: 195 calories
Fat: 15 g
Protein: 5 g
Carbohydrates: 14 g

Ingredients:
1 cup baby arugula
1 cup spinach
1 tbsp craisins
1 tbsp almonds, shaved or chopped
1 tbsps balsamic vinegar
½ tbsp extra virgin olive oil

Directions:

1) In a plate, mix arugula and spinach.
2) Top with craisins and almonds.
3) Drizzle olive oil and balsamic vinegar.
4) Serve and enjoy.

Cheese Quesadilla

Servings per Recipe: 1
Calories per Serving: 213 calories
Fat: 6 g
Protein: 13 g
Carbohydrates: 27 g

Ingredients:
1 whole grain tortilla
¼ cup cheese
1 tbsp Greek yogurt

Directions:

1) Place tortilla on a plate.
2) On the half side of tortilla spread the cheese. I use leftover cheese from my previous recipes. Sometimes I mix and match different cheeses which makes this recipe very versatile.
3) Fold in half tortilla and place in the oven toaster.
4) I bake it for around 5 minutes or until cheese is melted. You can also try to bake it longer, around 7 to 8 minutes if you want a crispier tortilla.

5) Remove tortilla from oven.
6) Slice it in wedges and serve with a dollop of Greek yogurt as a dipping sauce.
7) If you don't have yogurt you can use sour cream. Sometimes I improvise if I don't have any of these items in my pantry I add ½ tbsp lemon juice to ½ cup whipped cream and blend it on my food processor.

Fruity Asparagus-Quinoa Salad

Servings per Recipe: 8
Calories per Serving: 164
Fat: 6.3 g
Protein: 4.3 g
Carbohydrates: 24.7 g

Salad Ingredients:
½ jalapeno pepper, diced
½ lb asparagus, sliced to 2-inch lengths, steamed and chilled
5 dates, pitted and chopped
2 tbsps minced red onion
¼ cup chopped pecans, toasted
1 cup fresh orange sections
½ tsp kosher salt
2 cups water
1 cup uncooked quinoa
½ cup finely chopped white onion
1 tsp olive oil

Dressing Ingredients:
Mint sprigs – optional
2 tbsps chopped fresh mint
1 garlic clove, minced
¼ tsp ground black pepper
¼ tsp kosher salt
1 tbsp olive oil
2 tbsps fresh lemon juice

Directions:

1) Wash and rub with your hands quinoa in a bowl at least three times, discarding water each and every time.
2) On medium high fire, place a large nonstick fry pan and heat 1 tsp olive oil. For two minutes, sauté onions before adding quinoa and sautéing for another five minutes.
3) Add ½ tsp salt and 2 cups water and bring to a boil. Lower fire to a simmer, cover and cook for 15 minutes. Turn off fire and let stand until water is absorbed.
4) Add pepper, asparagus, dates, pecans and orange sections into a salad bowl. Add cooked quinoa, toss to mix well.
5) In a small bowl, whisk mint, garlic, black pepper, salt, olive oil and lemon juice to create the dressing.
6) Pour dressing over salad, serve and enjoy.

Potato Chowder

Servings per Recipe: 6
Calories per Serving: 247 calories
Fat: 6 g
Protein: 6 g
Carbohydrates: 43 g

Ingredients:
4 large potatoes, peeled and quartered
1 onion, sliced thinly
2 tbsps butter
Pepper and salt to taste
1 or 2 bacon rinds, cooked to a crisp and minced – optional
1 tbsp parsley, minced
½ cup Greek yogurt
1 tsp olive oil
2 cups water

Directions:

1) In a heavy bottomed pot, heat oil.
2) Add onions and sauté for 5 minutes or until soft and translucent.
3) Add butter and heat until melted.
4) Add quartered potatoes and water. Ensure that potatoes are halfway covered with water. Cover pot and bring to a boil, once boiling slow fire to a simmer.
5) Simmer potatoes until tender and mushy around 20 to 25 minutes.

6) Mashed the potatoes inside the pot with a ladle or puree with an immersion blender. I like mine with some bigger bits of potatoes so I hand mash it.
7) Season with pepper and salt to taste.
8) To make the chowder creamy, add Greek yogurt. Sometimes I also use sour cream or whipping cream—whichever I have in my ref.
9) You can add more water to make the chowder less thick or cook it some more to thicken the chowder.
10) Add bacon bits if using, stir to mix well.
11) Before serving, garnish with parsley.

Bread Dip and Topping Galore

Servings per Recipe: 6
Calories per Serving: 208 calories
Fat: 10 g
Protein: 6 g
Carbohydrates: 24 g

Ingredients:
¼ cup Balsamic Vinegar
¼ cup extra virgin olive oil
2 tbsps grated Parmesan Cheese or Asiago Cheese or combination
½ tsp pepper
½ tsp salt
1 ½ tsp Italian seasoning
2 cloves garlic minced
½ tbsp fresh basil, minced
6 medium tomatoes, seeds discarded and cubed

1 whole wheat French bread

Directions:

1) In medium bowl, mix balsamic vinegar, olive oil, cheese, pepper, salt, Italian seasoning, and garlic. Mix well and set aside for at least 30 minutes.
2) In another medium bowl, place cubed tomatoes.
3) Slice the whole wheat French bread diagonally at least an inch thick and place on a serving platter.
4) Once the dip has been set aside for at least 30 minutes, add the fresh basil before serving.
5) To eat, you can add tomatoes on top of the bread and drizzle with the dip. You can also dip your bread on the dipping sauce. Either way you want to enjoy this delicious feast.
6) You can even prepare the dip ahead of time and can be a quick pick me up snack.

Macaroni Soup

Servings per Recipe: 6
Calories per Serving: 169 calories
Fat: 3 g
Protein: 12 g
Carbohydrates: 23 g

Ingredients:
1 cup of minced beef or chicken or a combination of both
1 cup carrots, diced
1 cup milk

½ medium onion, sliced thinly
3 garlic cloves, minced
Salt and pepper to taste
2 cups broth (chicken, vegetable or beef)
½ tbsp olive oil
1 cup uncooked pasta like macaroni, shells, even angel hair broken to pieces
1 cup water

Directions:

1) In a heavy bottomed pot on medium high fire heat oil.
2) Add garlic and sauté for a minute or two until fragrant but not browned.
3) Add onions and sauté for 3 minutes or until soft and translucent.
4) Add a cup of minced meat. Sometimes I use whatever leftover frozen meat I have from ground beef or lamb or pork to chicken to those extra meat slices, I combine them all up. This is what clean eating is all about—not letting those food go to waste just because it's too few or small.
5) Sauté the meat well until cooked around 8 minutes. While sautéing, season meat with pepper and salt.
6) Add water and broth and bring to a boil.
7) Once boiling, add pasta. I use any leftover pasta that I have in the pantry. If all you have left is spaghetti, lasagna, angel hair or fettuccine, what I do is break them into pieces—around 1-inch in length before adding to the pot.

8) Slow fire to a simmer and cook while covered until pasta is soft.
9) Halfway through cooking the pasta, around 8 minutes I add the carrots.
10) Once the pasta is soft, turn off fire and add milk.
11) Mix well and season to taste again if needed.
12) Serve and enjoy.

Preview of "Fruit Fusion: Fruit Infused Smoothies for Ultimate Weight Loss and Detox (Fruit Infused Water Complimentary Edition)"

Chapter 3: Organic Produce VS Conventional Produce

When it comes to making smoothies, many people always recommend using organic and fresh products. However, before we delve on this topic further, it is important that we define what organic foods and conventional foods are.

According to the United States Department of Agriculture, organic foods are defined as produce that are grown and processed using sound farming methods that both recycle resources and promote biodiversity in the farmland. This means that organic produce are raised without using pesticides, petroleum-based fertilizers and others. On the other hand, animals that are raised using organic methods are fed with organic feeds, not given antibiotics and are given access to frolic outdoors. The thing is that organic produce refers to growing food in the most natural and traditional way possible as opposed to conventional produce.

Conventional produce, on the other hand, is the complete opposite of organic produce. Single crops are grown in massive plantations and farmers heavily rely on pesticides and fertilizers in order to increase the yield of their farm. In most cases, the fruits and vegetables that we see in big supermarkets are grown in conventional methods of farming.

The Benefits of Using Organic Foods

There are many conflicts revolving around the benefits of organic foods. Some people believe that organic and conventional foods are not different when it comes to the nutrients that they contain. However, many researchers have found out that choosing organic produce has many advantages. Below is the list of the benefits that you will get when it comes to choosing organic foods?

- They do not contain preservatives and additives that may be harmful to health.
- They contain higher levels of vitamins like Vitamin C, Magnesium, Iron and Phosphorus which are easily lost when they are processed.
- They are free from toxic residues from pesticides and inorganic fertilizers that can cause damage to the body especially the nervous system.

Sample Recipe: Detoxifying Super Green Smoothie

Every once in a while, love your body by undergoing detoxification with this super green smoothie. Try it, it tastes great!

Servings per recipe: 2
Nutritional Information per Serving
Calories: 160
Fat: 0 g
Carbs: 39 g
Protein: 3 g
Fiber: 5 g
Sodium: 56 mg

Ingredients:
¼ cup chopped fresh mint leaves
¼ cup chopped flat leaf parsley
1 cup chilled orange or tangerine juice
2 medium ribs celery, chopped
1 ¼ cups mango, frozen cubes
1 ¼ cup Kale, stems and ribs removed
1 medium cucumber, peeled
6 ice cubes
2-3 dates for sweetness – optional

Directions:

1) In a blender, combine all ingredients.
2) Pulse until you have a smooth consistency.
3) Equally pour into two serving glasses
4) Serve and enjoy.

[Click here to check out the rest of "Fruit Fusion: Fruit Infused Smoothies for Ultimate Weight Loss and Detox (Fruit Infused Water Complimentary Edition)" on Amazon.](http://bit.ly/fruitfusionsmoothies)

Or go to: http://bit.ly/fruitfusionsmoothies

Check Out My Other Books

Below you'll find some of my other recommended books that are popular on Amazon and Kindle as well. If you have the Kindle version, simply click on the links below to check them out. As part of the Kindle Matchbook Program, you can download your discounted Kindle eBook copy of this book if you own the print version. Simply login to your Amazon account, go to your orders history and purchase the Kindle discounted version. As an added bonus for Kindle owners, you'll get an instant Bonus Content section containing more clean eating tips, tricks and meal plans online.

Or, if you are happy with the print only version you can simply search for these titles in Amazon's search box. Alternatively, you can visit my author page on Amazon to see other work done by me.

Fruit Fusion: 25 Healthy & Delicious Infused Vitamin Water Recipes
Fruit Fusion Box Set: 25 Healthy & Delicious Fruit Infused Vitamin Water Recipes + Fruit Infused Smoothies for Weight Loss & Detox Cleanse
Growing Organic Berries: The Ultimate Guide to Naturally Growing the Most Delicious Berries at Home

If the links do not work, for whatever reason, you can simply search for these titles on the Amazon website to find them.

Printed in Great Britain
by Amazon.co.uk, Ltd.,
Marston Gate.